COOKIES
and
CAKES

Edited by Jane Solmson

WEATHERVANE BOOKS
New York

This edition is published by Weathervane Books,
    distributed by Crown Publishers, Inc.
a b c d e f g h

Published under arrangement with Ottenheimer Publishers, Inc.
Printed in the United States of America

CONTENTS

BAKING HINTS

When creaming butter and sugar, adding a little hot milk will aid in the creaming process.

An apple cut in half and placed in a cake box will keep cake fresh several days longer.

When making a cake, always add 2 tablespoons boiling water to butter and sugar mixture. This makes a fine-textured cake.

Do not grease the sides of cake pans. How would you like to climb a greased pole?

To cut a fresh cake, use a wet knife.

Do not discard rinds of grapefruit, oranges, or lemons. Grate rinds, put in tightly covered glass jar, and store in refrigerator. Makes excellent flavoring for cakes, frostings, and such.

Make a good, quick frosting by boiling a small potato, mashing it, and adding powdered sugar and vanilla.

To keep crisp cookies crisp and soft cookies soft, place only one kind in a jar.

A cake will be greatly improved if a teaspoon of lemon juice is added to the butter and sugar. This makes a cake very light and shorter. Fresh milk makes cakes close-grained and more solid.

For a nice decoration on white frosting, shave colored gumdrops very thin and stick on. They will curl like little roses.

Baking Pans: For best results use correct size of pan. The time and oven temperature should be adjusted to the type of pan being used. For shortening-type cakes, bake cupcakes at 375° 18 to 20 minutes; layer cakes at 350° 30 to 35 minutes, and loaf cakes at 350° 40 to 45 minutes.

Shortly before taking cupcakes from the oven, place a marshmallow on each for frosting.

Use a thread instead of a knife to cut a cake while it is still hot.

For super-easy-to-frost cakes, when you grease your pan, don't flour it. Put sugar on the sides and bottom. This will make a glaze on the bottom and the cake will not get crumbly when you frost it. If you are not going to frost your cake, it will keep it moist longer, because it gets hard on the outside.

If a little of the flour called for in a recipe is added to nut, raisins, candied fruits, et cetera, they will run through a grinder without sticking.

To prevent a cake from sticking to the plate, sprinkle the plate with powdered sugar.

What to do with leftover cake? Refrigerate or freeze it. Slice it; line bottoms of paper-lined muffin cups or sherbets with slices; cover with fruit, ice cream, or whip. Crumble cake and fold into puddings. Use as topping.

ROLLED COOKIES

Chocolate-Wine Cookies

1½ cups all-purpose flour
1 teaspoon baking powder
½ teaspoon cinnamon

Sift flour, baking powder, and cinnamon together onto clean working surface.
Shape into a ring.

1 egg, beaten
1 cup ground pecans
½ cup butter, softened
½ cup sugar
1 teaspoon sherry
1 6-ounce package chocolate chips, melted

Place egg, pecans, butter, sugar, sherry, and ½ cup chocolate in center.
Blend mixture with pastry scrapers until smooth dough is formed.
Roll out dough on floured surface to ⅛ inch thick.
Cut into circles with 1½-inch cookie cutter.
Press circles into miniature cupcake pans, forming very shallow shells.

Bake in preheated 350°F oven about 20 to 22 minutes.
Cool on wire rack.
Fill centers with remaining melted chocolate.

Almond slivers

Insert an almond sliver in each dab of chocolate.

Chill 5 minutes to set chocolate.

Yield: about 3½ dozen.

Butter Cookies

⅔ cup butter
1¼ cups sugar
2 eggs

Cream butter, sugar, and eggs together until light and foamy.

3 cups flour
1½ teaspoon salt
2 teaspoons baking powder
1 teaspoon vanilla

Sift flour, salt, and baking powder together; add to first mixture. Add vanilla.

Mix until smooth. Chill.
Roll to ¼-inch thickness, on slightly floured board. Cut with cookie cutter.
Sprinkle with sugar; bake in 350°F oven 12 to 15 minutes.

Yield: 60 cookies.

Pretzel Cookies

Pretzel Cookies

½ cup (1 stick) butter or
  margarine
¾ cup granulated sugar
2 eggs, beaten
2 tablespoons milk
1 cup flour
¼ teaspoon salt

½ cup brown sugar
2 tablespoons ground
  cinnamon

Preheat oven to 375°F.

Cream butter with ¼ cup granulated sugar.

Add eggs and milk; beat until smooth.

Add flour and salt sifted together; mix to smooth dough.

Wrap in foil.

Chill 2 to 3 hours.

Mix brown sugar, cinnamon, and remaining granulated
  sugar together.
Sprinkle mixture onto pastry board.
Put dough on board.
Roll out to about ¼ inch thick.
Cut dough into strips about ½ inch wide.
Form into twists.
Sprinkle well with sugar mixture.

Arrange on greased and floured baking sheets.

Bake 12 minutes or until just delicately browned.

Yield: about 36 cookies.

Peanut-Butter Cookies

2 cups sifted flour
1½ teaspoons baking
  powder
½ teaspoon salt

Sift flour, baking powder, and salt together.

2 tablespoons shortening
½ cup peanut butter
1 cup sugar
1 egg
1 teaspoon vanilla
⅓ cup milk

Cream shortening and peanut butter together.
Beat in other ingredients, except peanuts, one at a time.
Stir in flour mixture; blend well.

Chill.

Roll out to ¼-inch thick on slightly floured board.

Cut with cookie cutter.

½ cup chopped peanuts

Place on ungreased baking sheet. Sprinkle with peanuts.

Bake in 350°F oven 12 to 15 minutes.
Yield: 50 cookies.

Soft Ginger Cookies

5 cups sifted flour
4 teaspoons baking soda
½ teaspoon salt
2 teaspoons ginger
1½ teaspoons cinnamon
1½ teaspoons allspice

Mix and sift flour, soda, salt, and spices.

1¼ cups butter
⅓ cup brown sugar

Cream butter well.
Gradually add sugar.
Continue creaming until fluffy.
Add molasses and egg; mix well.

1½ cups dark molasses
1 egg, well beaten
½ cup boiling water

Add sifted ingredients alternately with water, mixing just
  enough after each addition to combine ingredients.
Chill dough.
Roll ⅛-inch thick on floured board.
Cut with assorted floured cutters.

Bake on ungreased cookie sheets in preheated 350°F oven
  about 15 minutes.
Decorate as desired.

Approximate Yield: about 6 dozen.

Fig Newtons

½ cup butter
1½ cups sugar

Cream butter and 1 cup sugar.

1 well-beaten egg

Add egg; beat until light.

½ cup milk
1 teaspoon vanilla

Mix milk and vanilla.

½ teaspoon salt
3 cups flour
3 teaspoons baking powder

Sift salt, flour, and baking powder together. Add alternately with milk to creamed mixture; blend well.

Roll out to ⅛-inch thick rectangle on slightly floured board.

1 cup chopped figs

Put figs in saucepan with remaining sugar and 1 cup boiling water; boil 5 minutes.
Cool.
Spread cooked mixture over ½ of dough.
Cover with uncovered half of dough.
Cut into oblongs.

Bake in 400°F oven 12 to 15 minutes.

Yield: about 4 dozen.

Cinnamon Graham Crackers

Suggestion: Let children help make these into "animal" crackers by cutting them out with animal-shaped cookie cutters. Don't forget to prick tops!

½ cup butter or margarine
⅔ cup brown sugar

Cream together butter and sugar.

1 teaspoon vanilla

Add vanilla; beat well.

1 cup all-purpose flour
2 cups whole-wheat flour
1 teaspoon baking powder
½ teaspoon baking soda
¼ teaspoon salt
1½ teaspoons cinnamon
½ to ⅔ cup milk

Stir together flours, baking powder, soda, salt, and cinnamon until well combined.
Add flour mixture alternately with milk to creamed mixture, adding just enough milk that mixture is consistency of pie dough and holds together.

Divide dough into thirds.
On floured board roll out each portion into ⅛-inch-thick rectangle.
Cut into squares (3 × 3 inches).

Place on greased baking sheets.
Prick each square thoroughly with fork.
Bake at 350°F 10 to 12 minutes, until edges are crisp and brown.

Yield: 3 dozen.

Cornflake Cookies

1 cup shortening
1½ cups sugar
2 well-beaten eggs
¼ cup milk
1 cup raisins

2 cups flour
2 teaspoons baking soda
2 cups cornflakes

Cream shortening and sugar.

Add eggs; beat until light.
Add milk and raisins.

Sift flour with baking soda; add, blending well.
Add cornflakes.
Roll to ¼-inch thick on slightly floured board.
Cut with a cookie cutter.
Place on baking sheet.

Bake in 350°F oven 12 to 15 minutes.

Yield: 48 cookies.

Nantes Cookies

1½ cups all-purpose flour
1 teaspoon baking powder
2 eggs, well beaten
½ cup butter, softened
½ cup sugar

2 tablespoons Basic Sugar Syrup

¼ cup finely chopped slivered almonds

Sift flour and baking powder together into a mound on a
    clean working surface. Shape into a ring.
Pour eggs into center. Add butter and sugar. Blend well
    with 2 pastry scrapers until smooth dough is formed.

Roll dough to ⅛ inch thick on lightly floured surface.

Cut with floured 1½-inch-round cutter.
Brush cookies with sugar syrup.
Sprinkle with almonds.

Make firm indentation in center of each cookie with finger.

Place cookies on buttered and floured cookie sheet.

Bake in preheated 350°F oven 18 to 20 minutes or until
    lightly browned.

Cool cookies on wire rack.

1 6-ounce package chocolate chips, melted

Drop small amount of melted chocolate onto center of
    each cookie, from demitasse spoon.

Chill cookies no longer than 5 minutes to set chocolate.

Yield: about 3½ dozen.

Basic Sugar Syrup

6 cups water
8½ cups sugar

Place water and sugar in large pot over low heat. Heat
    until sugar is dissolved. Raise to slow, rolling boil, then
    reduce temperature. Simmer 3 minutes.

Chill, bottle, and store.

Sugar Cookies

This is a basic cookie recipe and is very useful because there are endless variations. They all keep well if stored in a tightly covered cookie jar. (The basic recipe makes 50-60 cookies)

Preheat oven to 375°F.

2 cups flour (approximately)
1½ teaspoons baking powder
½ teaspoon salt

Sift 1½ cups of flour with baking powder and salt.

½ cup (1 stick) butter or other shortening
1 cup sugar
1 egg
1 teaspoon vanilla extract
1 tablespoon cream or milk

Cream butter until soft.

Beat in sugar, egg, vanilla, and cream.
Stir in the flour mixture.
Add enough remaining flour to make dough stiff enough to roll out.

Refrigerate until well chilled.

Place on lightly floured board.
Roll about ⅛ inch thick.
Cut into desired shapes with a floured cutter, or use a cookie press.

Place on ungreased baking sheets.

Sprinkle with sugar.

Bake 8 to 10 minutes.

Remove to cooling trays.

Cookies can be served plain or decorated in a variety of ways.

Sour-Cream Cookies
Reduce baking powder to ½ teaspoon.
Add ¼ teaspoon baking soda and ¼ teaspoon ground cinnamon or nutmeg to flour.
Substitute a squeeze of lemon juice for vanilla and ⅓ cup of sour cream for fresh cream.

Butterscotch Cookies
Substitute 1 cup brown sugar for white sugar.

Spice Sugar Cookies
Mix and sift ¼ teaspoon each ground cinnamon and powdered cloves with flour.
Omit vanilla.

Sugar Cookies

Rolled Spice Cookies

3¾ cups sifted flour 1¼ teaspoons baking powder 2½ teaspoons cinnamon 1¼ teaspoons cloves	Mix and sift flour, baking powder, and spices.
1½ cups butter 2 cups brown sugar 1 egg	Cream butter. Add sugar gradually; cream until fluffy. Add egg; mix. Add sifted ingredients gradually; mix. Chill thoroughly. Roll about ⅛ inch thick. Cut with assorted floured cutters. Bake on ungreased cookie sheets in preheated 350°F oven about 12 minutes. Decorate as desired. Yield: about 6 dozen.

Crispy Orange Cookies

For variety use lemon instead of orange or add 1 teaspoon mixed spice with the flour.

1¼ cups flour	Sift flour and ground rice into bowl.
¼ cup ground rice	
½ cup (1 stick) butter or margarine	Rub in butter until mixture resembles fine bread crumbs.
⅜ cup white sugar	Add sugar, orange rind, and egg yolk; mix well.
Grated rind of 1 large orange	Knead until smooth.
1 egg, separated	Wrap in foil.
	Refrigerate ½ hour.
	Roll out dough to about 12 inches square.
	Brush with lightly beaten egg white.
½ cup brown sugar	Sprinkle with brown sugar.
	Fold corners of dough to center. Form into a ball. Knead lightly.
	Cut in half.
	Shape each half into a roll about 9 inches long.
	Cut rolls into slices about ½ inch thick.
	Place on greased baking sheets.
	Bake about 20 minutes.
	Remove to cooling trays.
	Store when quite cold.
	Yield: about 36 cookies.

Crispy Orange Cookies

SHAPED COOKIES

Bright-Eyed Susans

Bright-Eyed Susans

2 cups flour **½ teaspoon baking powder**	Preheat oven to 350°F. Sift flour and baking powder twice.
1 cup butter or margarine **½ cup sugar** **2 tablespoons water** **1 teaspoon vanilla extract** **1 egg**	Cream butter and sugar until light and fluffy. Add water, vanilla, and egg yolk. Add flour; mix well.
1¼ cups finely chopped nuts	Form dough into balls about size of a walnut. Roll in slightly beaten egg white, then in nuts. Place on lightly greased baking sheets. Bake 5 minutes. Remove from oven. Press your thumb print in each ball. Return to oven.
A little jam or jelly	Bake 8 to 10 minutes. Remove to cooling trays. Fill centers with bright jam or jelly. Yield: about 48 cookies.

Chocolate Balls

3 squares unsweetened
  baking chocolate
1 tablespoon strong black
  coffee

1 cup (2 sticks) butter or
  margarine
¼ cup sugar
1 egg yolk
1 cup chopped walnuts or
  pecans
1 tablespoon rum
2½ cups flour

Preheat oven to 350°F.
Break chocolate into small pieces. Put with coffee into
  double boiler. Stir until melted.
Let cool.

Cream butter and sugar until light and fluffy.
Beat in egg yolk.
Add nuts and rum.
Stir in cooled chocolate.
Add sifted flour; blend to smooth dough.
Wrap in foil.
Chill 1 hour.
Form teaspoons of dough into balls.
Roll well in sugar.
Arrange on well-greased baking sheets, leaving space bet-
  ween for them to spread.
Press half a nut into each ball.

Bake about 15 minutes.

Yield: about 40 small cookies.

Chocolate Balls

Rich Chocolate Tea Cookies

2 cups sifted cake flour
½ teaspoon salt

½ cup butter
1 cup sugar
1 egg
2 squares (1 ounce each) unsweetened chocolate, melted, cooled
½ teaspoon vanilla extract
2 tablespoons milk

Mix and sift flour and salt.

Cream butter. Add sugar gradually; cream until fluffy.
Add egg and chocolate; mix well.

Add extract to milk.
Add sifted ingredients alternately with milk to chocolate mixture; mix just enough after each addition to combine ingredients.
Using cookie press, form into desired shapes on ungreased cookie sheets.
Decorate as desired with colored sugar, candy, nuts, candied fruit, etc.

Bake in preheated 400°F oven about 9 minutes.

Yield: about 6⅓ dozen.

Double Crunchers

1 cup sifted flour
½ teaspoon baking soda
¼ teaspoon salt

½ cup butter
½ cup granulated sugar
½ cup brown sugar
1 egg
½ teaspoon vanilla extract
1 cup crushed cornflakes
1 cup oats, uncooked
½ cup chopped nuts

Mix and sift flour, baking soda, and salt.

Cream butter.
Add sugars; mix well. Beat until light and creamy.
Blend in egg and extract.
Stir in flour mixture.
Add cornflakes, oats, and nuts.
Remove ⅓ of dough.
Shape into balls, using level half-teaspoonfuls of dough.
Place on greased cookie sheet.
Flatten with bottom of glass dipped in flour.
Bake in preheated 350°F oven 8 to 9 minutes.
Using remaining ⅔ dough, shape into balls, using level teaspoonfuls, flattening as above.
Bake 10 to 11 minutes.
Cool.

Chocolate Cream-Cheese Filling

1 package (6 ounces) semi-sweet chocolate bits
½ cup sifted confectioners' sugar
1 tablespoon water
1 package (3 ounces) cream cheese, softened

Spread filling over large cookie; top with small one.

Yield: 7½ dozen.
Melt chocolate with sugar and water.

Blend in cream cheese; beat until smooth.
Cool.

Galettes

Very good served with coffee. Lemon rind can be omitted and a variety of alternative flavorings used. (Makes about 20 cookies)

2 cups flour
½ teaspoon salt

Preheat oven to 350°F.
Sift flour and salt together.

⅓ cup butter or margarine
½ cup sugar
2 eggs
Grated rind of 1 lemon

Beat butter and sugar until light and creamy.
Add eggs one at a time; beat well after each addition.
Stir in flour and lemon rind.
Put spoonful of dough on well-floured board.
Using your hands, form into roll about 6 inches long.
Fold roll in half.
Twist the two halves around each other.
Repeat with remaining dough.
Arrange on greased baking sheet.
Brush with beaten egg or sweetened milk.

Bake 20 minutes or until golden brown.

Anise Galettes

Omit lemon rind.
Add few drops of anise flavoring to creamed mixture.

Cinnamon Galettes

Omit lemon rind.
Add ½ teaspoon ground cinnamon with the flour.

Maryses Fingers

1 cup butter, softened
½ cup sifted confectioners' sugar
1½ cups all-purpose flour

Place butter into large mixing bowl; cream with electric mixer until light and smooth.
Add sugar; mix until blended.
Add flour gradually, mixing to stiff dough.

Place dough in pastry bag with large star tube affixed.
Pipe dough into 3-inch lengths onto buttered and floured baking sheet.

Bake in preheated 375°F oven about 10 minutes or until golden brown.

Remove from baking sheet.
Place on rack to cool.

Yield: about 5 dozen.

Gingersnaps

2¼ cups sifted flour
2 teaspoons baking soda
½ teaspoon salt
1 teaspoon ginger
1 teaspoon cinnamon
½ teaspoon ground cloves

Mix and sift flour, soda, salt, ginger, cinnamon, and cloves.

¾ cup shortening
1 cup sugar
¼ cup molasses
1 egg
3 tablespoons sugar
Water

Cream shortening.
Add 1 cup sugar gradually; cream until fluffy.
Add molasses; mix. Add egg; mix.
Add sifted ingredients gradually; mix.
Allowing 1 tablespoon dough for each cookie, shape into ball.
Dip top of cookie into remaining sugar.
Top with drop of water.
Place on ungreased cookie sheets.

Bake in preheated 375°F oven about 10 minutes.

Yield: 3½ dozen.

Chocolate-Topped Macaroons

1 cup sugar
1 8-ounce can almond paste
2 egg whites

Combine sugar and almond paste in large bowl; mix with fingers until well blended.
Add egg whites gradually (just enough to moisten), mixing with wooden spoon.
Roll lightly into walnut-sized balls; flatten slightly.
Place about 2 inches apart on brown paper on baking sheet.

Bake in preheated 325°F oven about 12 minutes or until very lightly browned.
Remove from oven.
Slide paper onto damp towel.
Cool slightly, then remove macaroons with a spatula.

Yield: about 2 dozen.

Chocolate Topping

Chocolate chips, melted
24 candied cherries
¼ cup sugar

Spread each macaroon with chocolate.

Roll cherries in sugar; press into chocolate.
Put in refrigerator no longer than 5 minutes for chocolate to set.

DROP COOKIES

Easy Macaroons

2 eggs
⅔ cup sugar
½ teaspoon almond extract
1 (8-ounce) package
   shredded coconut

Beat eggs slightly in mixing bowl.
Add sugar, almond extract, and coconut; stir to mix
   thoroughly.
Drop mixture by heaping teaspoonfuls onto well-greased
   baking sheet.
Bake at 350°F 12 minutes or until lightly browned.
Cool on wire rack.

Yield: about 3 dozen.

Sweet Chocolate Drops

⅓ cup sifted flour
¼ teaspoon baking powder
¼ teaspoon cinnamon
⅛ teaspoon salt

Mix and sift flour, baking powder, cinnamon, and salt.

2 bars (4 ounces each) sweet
   chocolate
1 tablespoon butter

Melt chocolate and butter together. Cool.

2 eggs
¾ cup sugar
½ teaspoon vanilla extract
¾ cup finely chopped
   pecans

Beat eggs until foamy.
Add sugar, 2 tablespoons at a time, to eggs; beat until
   thickened (about 5 minutes).
Blend in chocolate mixture.
Add flour mixture; blend well.
Stir in extract and pecans.

Drop by teaspoonfuls onto greased cookie sheet.

Bake in preheated 350°F oven about 10 minutes. Cookies
   should feel "set" when lightly touched.

Cool slightly before removing from cookie sheet.
Yield: 9 dozen.

Coconut Macaroons

Coconut Macaroons, with their crisp-chewy outsides and soft centers, are popular with children and grown-ups alike.

4 egg whites
1 teaspoon vanilla extract
1 cup confectioners' sugar

2 cups flaked coconut
½ cup all-purpose flour

Beat egg whites with electric mixer until stiff peaks form. Add vanilla; mix well.
Gradually add confectioners' sugar; beat well after each addition. Beat until stiff and glossy.
Fold in the coconut and flour; mix well.

Drop from teaspoon onto buttered and floured cookie sheet.

Bake in preheated 325°F oven 25 minutes or until lightly browned.

Yield: 2 dozen macaroons.

Coconut Macaroons

Cornflake Kisses

Preheat oven to 300°F.

Line 2 cookie sheets with aluminum foil. Grease foil.

2 egg whites
¼ teaspoon salt
½ teaspoon cream of tartar
½ cup sugar

½ cup shredded coconut
½ cup chocolate chips
1½ cups cornflakes
  (not crumbs)
1 teaspoon vanilla
¼ teaspoon almond extract

Beat egg whites until foamy. Sprinkle with salt and cream of tartar. Continue beating until thick.

Gradually add sugar about a tablespoon at a time until stiff meringue is formed.
Fold in coconut, chocolate, cornflakes, and flavorings by hand.

Drop by heaping teaspoonfuls onto lined cookie sheets.

Bake 20 to 25 minutes.

Yield: 3 dozen.

Cherry Kisses

3 egg whites
⅛ teaspoon salt
½ teaspoon cream of tartar
2¼ cups sifted confec-
    tioners' sugar
1 teaspoon vanilla extract
Food color (optional)
1 cup chopped pecans
¾ cup finely chopped
    candied cherries

Beat egg whites, salt, and cream of tartar until firm peaks are formed.

Add sugar gradually, while beating. Add extract and coloring; mix well.

Fold in nuts and cherries.

Drop by spoonfuls onto lightly greased cookie sheets. Bake in preheated 275°F oven 15 to 20 minutes.

Yield: approximately 5 dozen.

Florentines

Preheat oven to 375°F.
Grease some baking sheets. Line with greased paper; dust lightly with cornstarch.

¼ cup sultana raisins
2 cups crushed cornflakes
¼ cup peanuts
½ cup candied or
    maraschino cherries
½ cup condensed milk
3 squares baking chocolate

Mix raisins, cornflakes, peanuts, and cherries together in a mixing bowl.

Add milk; blend well.
Place mixture by 2 teaspoonfuls in small heaps on sheets.
Bake 15 to 20 minutes.
Leave on sheets to cool. Using spatula, remove to cooling trays.
Melt chocolate in double boiler.
Remove from heat; stir until slightly thickened.
Spread over flat sides of cookies, mark with a fork.
Let chocolate set before storing.

Yield: 30 cookies.

Florentines

Peanut-Butter Nuggets

Peanut-Butter Nuggets

These little cookies are very quickly made and are generally very popular with children. They are ideal for parties.

1 cup peanut butter
1 teaspoon lemon juice
¼ teaspoon salt
1½ cups (1 can) condensed milk
1 cup chopped seedless raisins

Preheat oven to 375°F.
Mix peanut butter, lemon juice, and salt together.

Gradually stir in milk.

Add raisins.
Drop by teaspoon onto greased baking sheets.

Bake 10 minutes.

Yield: about 36.

SKILLET AND UNCOOKED COOKIES

Grandmother Cookies

Little hands can help shape them—fun for everybody. Eat them all up—they're too good to store.

½ cup margarine
½ cup sugar
2 eggs

Cream together margarine, sugar, and eggs until smooth.

2 cups flour
2 teaspoons baking powder
1 teaspoon salt
1½ teaspoons cinnamon
½ cup raisins (optional)

Combine dry ingredients.
Add to egg mixture.

Add raisins.
Batter will be stiff and buttery.

Take a teaspoonful, roll it between your palms, and flatten it to the size of a 2-inch circle.

Put into lightly greased skillet.
When cookie puffs up, turn it once; brown other side.

Yield: 3 dozen plus.

Apricot Balls

1 cup dried apricots
½ cup walnuts
½ cup coconut
2 tablespoons wheat germ
4 tablespoons orange juice
⅓ cup finely chopped walnuts

Put apricots, ½ cup walnuts, and coconut through food grinder.

Add wheat germ and orange juice; mix well.
Form into 1-inch balls.
Roll in chopped walnuts.
Refrigerate.

Yield: 20 to 24 balls.

Walnut Rum Cookies

Very fast and easy.

1 cup chopped walnuts	Mix all ingredients except sugar.
2 tablespoons cocoa	Form into balls.
¼ cup rum or bourbon	
2 cups finely crushed vanilla wafers	
3 tablespoons white corn syrup	
2 cups confectioners' sugar	Roll in sugar.
	Yield: 30 to 35 cookies.

Hartshorns

This two-part recipe is worth the trouble. Hartshorns store well and can be made ahead.

¼ pound butter or margarine	Melt butter. Let cool.
4 eggs	Beat eggs and sugar together.
1 cup sugar	Add butter, lemon rind, cardamom, baking soda, and flour; mix well.
½ lemon rind, grated	
½ teaspoon ground cardamom	Place in refrigerator to chill overnight.
2 teaspoons baking soda	
4½ cups flour	Roll small lumps of dough into strips 6 inches long and as thick as your little finger.
Fat for deep frying	Form each strip into a ring.
	Cook rings in deep fat until golden brown.
	Drain well on paper towels. Store in sealed tin.
	Yield: 36 hartshorns.

BAR COOKIES

Brownies

These are moist and keep well.

½ **pound butter** **4 squares bitter chocolate**	Melt butter and chocolate together.
2 cups sugar **4 eggs** ¼ **teaspoon salt**	At high speed beat sugar, eggs, and salt until well blended.
1 cup flour **2 teaspoons vanilla** **1 cup chopped nuts**	Add melted butter and chocolate. At low speed add flour and vanilla until well blended. Add nuts; mix.

Pour into 13 × 8½-inch baking pan.

Bake at 300°F 40 minutes or until tester comes out clean.

Cool.
Cut into squares.

Yield: 2 dozen.

Brownie Frosting

2 squares chocolate **3 tablespoons hot water** **1 tablespoon butter**	Melt chocolate with hot water over boiling water. Blend in butter. Cool.
2 cups sifted confectioners' **sugar** ½ **teaspoon vanilla**	Add sugar and vanilla.
1 egg	Beat in egg. Spread on cooled brownies. Sprinkle with nuts.

Butterscotch Brownies

¼ cup butter	Melt butter.
1 cup light brown sugar	Combine with brown sugar.
	Cool.
1 egg	Stir in egg and sifted dry ingredients.
¾ cup sifted flour	
1 teaspoon baking powder	
½ teaspoon salt	
½ teaspoon vanilla	Add vanilla and nuts.
½ cup chopped walnuts	
	Spread in well-greased 8-inch-square pan.
	Bake in 350°F oven 20 to 25 minutes.
	Cut into 1½ dozen bars while still warm.
	Yield: 1½ dozen.

Easy Layer Bars

½ cup melted butter	Pour butter into 13 × 9 × 2-inch pan.
1 cup graham-cracker	Sprinkle each of remaining ingredients in layers over top.
crumbs (about 15 cracker	
squares)	Bake in preheated 375°F oven about 25 minutes.
1 can (3½ ounces) flaked	
coconut	Cool about 1 hour.
1 package (6 ounces)	
semisweet chocolate bits	Cut into bars.
1 package (6 ounces) but-	
terscotch bits	Yield: 4 dozen.
1 cup chopped nuts	
1 can (15 ounces) sweetened	
condensed milk	

Congo Squares

1 pound brown sugar	Beat brown sugar and eggs.
3 eggs	
3 cups Bisquick	Add Bisquick; mix well.
1 small bag chocolate chips	Add chocolate chips and vanilla.
1 teaspoon vanilla	
	Put into greased 12 × 8-inch pan.
	Bake at 325°F 30 minutes.
	Cut into squares while still warm.
	Yield: 2 dozen.

Toffee Bars

½ pound butter
1 cup brown sugar
1 teaspoon vanilla
1 egg
¼ teaspoon salt

Mix together butter, sugar, vanilla, egg, and salt.

Bake in 8-inch-square pan in 350°F oven 20 to 25 minutes.

1 (6-ounce) package
  chocolate chips
¾ cup chopped nuts

Sprinkle with chocolate chips while warm; spread.
Sprinkle nuts evenly.

Cool.
Cut into squares.

Yield: 1 dozen.

Chocolate-Delight Bars

½ cup butter
1 egg yolk
2 tablespoons water
1¼ cups flour
1 teaspoon sugar
1 teaspoon baking powder

Beat together ½ cup butter, egg yolk, and water. Sift and
    stir in flour, sugar, and baking powder.
Press into 13 × 9 × 2-inch greased pan.

Bake at 350°F 10 minutes.

1 (12-ounce) package
  chocolate morsels

Remove from oven.
Sprinkle with morsels.
Return to oven 1 minute.

Remove.

Spread chocolate over top.

2 eggs
¾ cup sugar
6 tablespoons butter
2 teaspoons vanilla

Beat 2 eggs until thick.
Beat in ¾ cup sugar.
Stir in 6 tablespoons melted butter and vanilla.

2 cups finely chopped nuts

Spread on top of chocolate layer.
Sprinkle chopped nuts on top.

Bake at 350°F 30 to 35 minutes. Cut into 1½ inch squares.

Yield: 2 dozen.

Holiday Triangles

1 cup chopped pecans
½ cup candied fruit

Mix pecans and fruit.

1¼ cups all-purpose white
  flour
½ cup whole-wheat flour
½ teaspoon baking soda
½ teaspoon salt
½ teaspoon ground cloves
½ teaspoon allspice
½ teaspoon nutmeg
1 teaspoon cinnamon

Combine flours, soda, salt, and spices.
Sprinkle over fruit-and-nut mixture.

½ cup butter
¼ cup brown sugar, packed
1 egg, beaten
⅓ cup honey
2 tablespoons buttermilk

Cream butter and brown sugar until fluffy.

Beat in egg.
Add honey and buttermilk alternately with flour-and-nut
  mixture; mix well.

1 recipe Bourbon Glaze
Multicolored candy
  sprinkles

Spread batter on greased jelly-roll pan. Bake in preheated
  375°F oven 15 minutes or until done.

Remove from oven.

Frost with Bourbon Glaze.
Sprinkle with candy sprinkles.

Cut into triangular bars.

Remove from pan while still warm.

Yield: 2 dozen.

Holiday Triangles

Bourbon Glaze

2 tablespoons bourbon
2 tablespoons water
1 teaspoon vanilla
1 cup powdered sugar, sifted

Combine all ingredients;
  mix well.

Yield: approximately 1 cup.

REFRIGERATOR COOKIES

Almond Triangles

Almond Triangles are not only delicious but extremely attractive. These flaky cookies have been brushed with beaten eggs and sprinkled with chopped almonds. They are shown here in the shape of triangles, but they can be baked in other desired shapes.

½ cup butter
1 cup sugar
Combine butter and sugar in mixer bowl; cream until smooth.

6 tablespoons whipping cream
Beat in cream and 2 eggs.

3 eggs
½ teaspoon salt
2 cups flour
Add salt and flour; blend well.

Wrap in waxed paper and chill overnight.

Roll out on lightly floured surface.
Cut into triangles.

Beat the remaining egg slightly; brush over top surfaces of triangles.

Chopped almonds
Sprinkle with almonds.

Place triangles on greased baking sheet.

Bake in preheated 375°F oven 8 to 10 minutes or until golden brown.

Yield: 3 to 4 dozen.

Almond Triangles

Nutmeg Refrigerator Cookies

Nutmeg Refrigerator Cookies

Nutmeg and orange juice add spice and flavor to these crisp, flaky cookies. The convenience of make-ahead, bake-when-needed dough is part of their appeal. If desired, these cookies can be iced or dusted with confectioners' sugar.

½ cup butter ½ cup sugar	Cream butter with sugar in bowl.
6 tablespoons half-and-half cream 3 tablespoons orange juice Grated rind of 1 orange	Combine the cream, orange juice and rind; blend well.
3 cups all-purpose flour 1½ teaspoons nutmeg ½ teaspoon salt	Sift flour with nutmeg and salt. Add to butter mixture alternately with orange juice mixture. Add more flour, if needed, to form stiff dough.
	Shape into roll.
	Wrap in waxed paper.
	Chill overnight.
	Slice ⅛ inch thick. Cut small hole with piping tube or thimble in one side of each cookie.
	Place on greased baking sheet.
	Bake in preheated 375°F oven 8 to 10 minutes or until lightly browned. Yield: 4 to 5 dozen cookies.

Brown-Sugar Cookies

7 cups sifted flour
1 tablespoon soda
1 tablespoon cream of tartar
4 cups brown sugar
1 cup melted butter
4 eggs

Mix ingredients well.
Form into roll.
Let stand in refrigerator until firm—12 to 24 hours.
Slice.
Bake at 400°F 8 to 10 minutes or until lightly browned.
Yield: 100 cookies.

Crisp Coconut Refrigerator Cookies

1¾ cups plus 2 tablespoons sifted flour
1½ teaspoons baking powder
⅛ teaspoon salt
1 cup dry shredded coconut
1 egg
1 egg yolk
¾ cup sugar
1½ teaspoons vanilla extract
¾ cup melted butter

Mix and sift flour, baking powder, and salt.
Add coconut; mix well.

Beat egg and egg yolk until light.
Add sugar gradually; beat until fluffy.
Add extract.
Add flour mixture alternately with melted butter; after each addition mix just enough to combine ingredients.

Form dough into 2 rolls about 2 inches in diameter.
Chill thoroughly—12 to 24 hours.
Slice thin.
Bake on cookie sheets in preheated 400°F oven about 6 minutes.
Yield: about 6 dozen.

St. Nikalaas Cookies

½ cup butter or margarine
½ cup shortening
1 cup sugar
2 cups flour
2 teaspoons cinnamon
¼ teaspoon nutmeg
¼ teaspoon cloves
¼ teaspoon soda added to
    ¼ cup sour milk
¼ cup chopped nuts

Cream butter, shortening, and sugar.

Sift flour and spices together.

Add alternately with sour milk to creamed mixture.
Add nuts; mix well.

Knead into one or more loaves, depending on size cookies desired.
Store overnight in refrigerator.
Slice.

Bake at 375°F about 10 to 12 minutes.
Yield: about 5 dozen.

SINGLE-LAYER OR PAN CAKES

Apple Cake

4 cups chopped apples
½ cup salad oil
2 cups sugar
1 teaspoon vanilla
2 eggs

2 cups flour
1 teaspoon salt
1 heaping teaspoon baking soda
2 teaspoons cinnamon

Mix apples, oil, sugar, vanilla, and eggs together completely.

Add flour, salt, soda, and cinnamon.

Spread in 8 × 12-inch pan.
Bake 1 hour at 350°F.
If desired, sprinkle finished cake with powdered sugar.

Yield: 8 × 12-inch cake.

Applesauce Cake

¼ pound butter
3 cups bread crumbs
3 tablespoons sugar
2 teaspoons cinnamon

2 cups applesauce
2 tablespoons butter

Melt ¼ pound butter in pan.
Add bread crumbs, sugar, and cinnamon; stir until well mixed and golden brown.

Place ⅓ of bread-crumb mixture in well-greased deep-dish pie pan.
Cover with 1 cup applesauce.
Continue to layer with another ⅓ bread crumbs and another cup of applesauce.
Put rest of bread crumbs on top.
Dot with butter.

Bake at 375°F 25 minutes.

Serve cake at room temperature.

Yield: 6 to 8 servings.

Gingerbread

2 cups sifted cake flour
2 teaspoons baking powder
¼ teaspoon baking soda
2 teaspoons ginger
1 teaspoon cinnamon
½ teaspoon salt

⅓ cup shortening
½ cup sugar
1 egg, well beaten
⅔ cup molasses
¾ cup sour milk or
    buttermilk

12 marshmallows

Sift flour once; measure.
Add baking powder, soda, spices, and salt; sift together 3
    times.

Cream shortening thoroughly.
Add sugar gradually; cream together until light and fluffy.
Add egg and molasses.
Add flour alternately with milk; beat until smooth after
    each addition.

Pour into greased pan or ring mold.

Bake in 350°F oven 1¼ hours.

Serve with whipped cream.

As a variation use gingerbread as the base for fruit short-
    cakes.
Yield: 6 servings.

Butterscotch Cake with Marshmallows

1¾ cups flour
2 teaspoons baking powder
1 teaspoon salt

½ cup shortening
1½ cups brown sugar
¼ cup water
1 teaspoon vanilla
2 eggs
¼ cup milk

Sift flour; measure.
Sift again with baking powder and salt.

Mix shortening, sugar, and water.

Cook over low heat until sugar is dissolved; cool.
Add vanilla.
Add eggs one at a time, beating well after each addition.
Alternately add sifted dry ingredients and milk.
Beat until smooth, being careful not to overbeat.

Pour into 9-inch cake pan lined with paper.
Place marshmallows at intervals on top of batter.

Bake in 350°F oven 50 minutes.

Yield: 9-inch cake.

Peach Cake

1 cup sugar
½ cup butter
2 eggs
1 cup flour
1 teaspoon baking powder
Pinch of salt

2 medium-size cans sliced
  peaches, drained
2 tablespoons sugar
Cinnamon

Cream 1 cup sugar and butter.

Add eggs.
Add flour, baking powder, and salt.

Grease and flour 8 × 8-inch glass or springform pan.
Add batter. Overlap peaches on top of batter.
Sprinkle a little flour on top of peaches.
Sprinkle 2 tablespoons sugar over that. Heavily sprinkle
  cinnamon over everything.

Bake 1 hour at 350°F.

Yield: 8 × 8-inch cake.

Cherry Cake with Hot Cherry Sauce

⅓ cup shortening
1½ cups sugar
2 eggs, well beaten

2¼ cups flour
1½ teaspoons baking
  powder
½ teaspoon baking soda
½ teaspoon salt
1 cup milk
2 to 2¼ cups (No. 2 can)
  sour pitted cherries,
  well drained
½ cup chopped nuts

Hot Cherry Sauce

½ cup sugar
Dash of salt
2 tablespoons cornstarch
¾ cup cherry juice
1 cup water

¼ teaspoon almond
  flavoring

Cream shortening.
Add sugar gradually; cream until fluffy.
Blend in eggs.

Sift flour, baking powder, soda, and salt; stir into creamed
  mixture alternately with milk.

Blend in cherries and nuts.

Bake in greased 8 × 12-inch pan about 50 minutes at
  350°F. Serve warm with Hot Cherry Sauce.

Mix sugar, salt, and cornstarch together in saucepan.

Blend in cherry juice and water.
Boil until mixture thickens, about 10 minutes.
Remove from heat.
Blend in almond flavoring.

Serve hot over Cherry Cake.

Yield: 8 × 12-inch cake.

LAYER CAKES

Cherry Delight

1 package black-cherry gelatin	Prepare gelatin as directed.
1 cup pitted sweetened bing cherries	Stir in 1 cup cherries. Pour into 9-inch cake pan. Chill until firm.
1 quart vanilla ice cream, softened	Mold ice cream in 9-inch cake pan; chill until firm.
1¼ cups vanilla-wafer crumbs **6 tablespoons butter, melted**	Combine cookie crumbs and butter; work until all crumbs are moistened. Divide crumbs into 3 equal parts.
	Just prior to serving, assemble cake in following manner: Spread ⅓ of crumb mixture on serving platter. Unmold gelatin; place on top of crumb mixture on serving platter. Spread second portion of crumbs on top of gelatin. Unmold ice cream; place on top of crumb-topped gelatin. Spread remaining crumbs on top of ice cream.
1 cup powdered sugar **2 tablespoons cherry juice**	Combine powdered sugar and cherry juice; stir until smooth. Pour over top layer of crumbs.
2 cups whipped cream	Frost sides of cake with whipped cream. Score top of cake to indicate serving pieces.
12 whole canned bing cherries, pitted	Decorate each piece with a whipped-cream rosette and bing cherry. Yield: 12 servings.

Violet Garden

1 8-ounce spice-cake mix	Prepare cake. Bake in 1½-quart greased and floured ovenproof mixing bowl at 350°F 30 minutes or until done. Remove from bowl; cool.
5 to 6 drops green food coloring **1 9-ounce container whipped topping**	Fold food coloring into whipped topping until topping is evenly tinted. Fill pastry bag with whipped topping. Using rosette tip, cover cooled cake with whipped-topping rosettes, as illustrated.
2 dozen crystallized violets	Arrange crystal violets randomly over frosted cake. Refrigerate at least 2 hours to set before serving. Yield: 8 servings.

Violet Garden

Pineapple Upside-Down Cake

¼ cup butter **½ cup brown sugar** **2 tablespoons syrup from pineapple slices**	Melt butter in 9-inch-round cake pan. Stir in brown sugar and syrup.
1 can pineapple slices, drained	Arrange pineapple slices in sugar mixture.
Maraschino cherries, drained **1 small package white or yellow cake mix (enough for 1 layer), mixed**	Put cherries in holes. Pour cake batter over all. Bake in 350°F oven 45 minutes. Cool 5 minutes. Loosen edges; cover with plate; invert. Yield: 10 servings.

Sweetheart Cake

Sweetheart Cake

½ cup margarine
2 cups sugar
3 egg yolks

Cream margarine and sugar until light and fluffy.
Beat in egg yolks.

2 cups all-purpose flour
3 teaspoons baking powder
1 cup milk
1 teaspoon vanilla
3 egg whites, stiffly beaten

Combine flour and baking powder. Add to creamed mixture alternately with 1 cup milk; beat well after each addition.
Stir in vanilla.

Pour batter into 2 greased and floured heart-shaped pans. Bake at 350°F 35 minutes or until done.
Cool; remove from pans.

1 recipe Fluffy White Frosting (see Index)

Prepare frosting as directed.
Frost cake.

1 cup flaked coconut
1 teaspoon milk
2 to 3 drops red food coloring

Pour coconut, 1 teaspoon milk, and food coloring into small jar. Close jar; shake vigorously to tint coconut.

Decorate outer edge of cake with tinted coconut, as illustrated.

Yield: 12 servings.

Jam Cake

Preheat oven to 350°F.

1¾ cups sifted cake flour
¾ teaspoon baking powder
⅛ teaspoon salt

Sift together flour, baking powder, and salt; set aside.

Grease and flour 2 8-inch cake pans; line with waxed paper.

4 eggs (room temperature)
¾ cup granulated sugar
1 teaspoon grated lemon rind
½ teaspoon lemon extract

In large mixing bowl beat eggs until thick and lemon-colored.
Gradually beat in sugar. Mixture should be thick and light.
Using spatula, fold in flour mixture, lemon rind, and lemon extract.

Spread in prepared cake pans.
Bake 20 to 25 minutes or until toothpick inserted in center comes out clean.

Cool slightly.
Turn out onto rack; remove paper immediately.
Cool completely.

Center one layer on serving plate.

1 cup strawberry, raspberry, or blueberry jam
Confectioners' sugar

Spread with jam; top with second layer.

Top with sifted confectioners' sugar.

Yield: 6 servings.

Jam Cake

Crown Jewels

Crown Jewels

A dessert fit for a royal family.

1 cup all-purpose white flour 1 cup whole-wheat flour 2 teaspoons baking powder 1½ teaspoons baking soda ½ teaspoon salt 2 teaspoons apple-pie spice 1 cup granulated sugar	Combine flours, baking powder, soda, salt, and apple-pie spice.
1 cup brown sugar 1½ cups oil 4 eggs, beaten	Add sugars, oil, and eggs. Mix with electric beater 2 minutes.
2 cups grated carrots 1 8½-ounce can crushed pineapple, drained ½ cup chopped almonds	Add carrots, pineapple, and chopped nuts; stir in. Pour into 2 greased and floured 9-inch cake pans. Bake at 350°F 35 to 40 minutes or until done. Cool; remove from pans.
2 cups powdered sugar, sifted 2 to 3 tablespoons hot milk	Combine powdered sugar and enough hot milk to form a pourable icing; mix until smooth. Spread small amount of icing between layers; stack layers. Drizzle remaining icing over top and sides of cake.
½ cup candied fruit ½ cup slivered almonds	Combine fruit and slivered almonds. Sprinkle over top of cake.
	Yield: 12 servings.

38

Feather Devil's-Food Cake

½ cup shortening
1 cup white sugar
1 cup brown sugar

Thoroughly cream shortening and sugars.

2 eggs
1 teaspoon vanilla extract

Add eggs and vanilla; beat until fluffy.

3 (1-ounce) squares bitter
    chocolate
½ cup hot water

Melt chocolate in hot water over low heat; blend
    thoroughly; cool slightly. Add to creamed mixture.

2 cups cake flour
¼ teaspoon salt
1 teaspoon baking soda
⅔ cup milk

Sift dry ingredients 3 times.
Add alternately with milk, blending completely after each
    addition.
Place batter in 2 waxed-paper-lined 9-inch-round layer-cake
    pans.

Bake in 350°F oven 30 to 35 minutes.
Frost when cold with Chocolate Frosting (see Index).

Yield: 9-inch layer cake.

Whipped-Cream Torte

10 egg whites
1⅓ cups sugar
2 teaspoons vanilla
1⅓ cups finely ground
    blanched almonds

Beat egg whites until stiff but not dry.
Beat in 1⅓ cups sugar, small amount at a time.
Beat in 1 teaspoon vanilla.
Fold in ground almonds.

Pour into 2 greased and floured 10-inch cake pans.

Bake at 325°F 50 minutes.
Cool; remove from pans.

10 egg yolks

Place egg yolks in top of double boiler; beat vigorously
    over boiling water until creamy.

½ cup sugar
¼ teaspoon salt

Stir in ½ cup sugar and salt.
Remove from heat; cool.

1 cup margarine

Cream margarine until soft; stir into egg mixture.
Mix in 1 teaspoon vanilla.

Spread cooled filling between torte layers.

3 cups whipped cream

Spread whipped cream on sides and top of torte.
Decorate top with whipped-cream rosettes.

12 fresh raspberries
1 cup toasted almonds

Top each rosette with a whole raspberry.
Press almonds onto sides of torte.
Refrigerate.

Yield: 12 servings.

Fudge and Cream Layers

4 ounces unsweetened
   chocolate
½ cup boiling water
2 cups granulated sugar

Shave chocolate into double boiler.
Cover with boiling water; stir until chocolate melts and
   mixture thickens.
Add ½ cup sugar; cook and stir 2 minutes.
Cool to lukewarm.

2 cups all-purpose white
   flour
1 teaspoon baking soda
1 teaspoon salt

Combine flour, baking soda, and salt.

Cream margarine and 1¼ cups sugar until light and fluffy.
Add eggs one at a time, beating thoroughly after each
   addition.

½ cup margarine
3 eggs
⅔ cup milk
2 teaspoons vanilla

Add dry ingredients alternately with milk, starting and end-
   ing with dry ingredients; beat to blend, after each addition.
Add 1 teaspoon vanilla, then chocolate mixture; blend.

Pour batter into 2 greased and floured 9-inch pans.

Bake in 350°F oven 30 minutes or until cake has pulled
   away from sides of pan. Cool.

1 pint whipping cream

Whip cream until stiff.
Fold in ¼ cup sugar and 1 teapsoon vanilla.

Using thread and gentle sawing motion, or using sharp, thin
   knife, cut each layer in two.
Spread whipped cream between layers and over top and
   sides.

Chill until serving time.

Yield: 9-inch layer cake.

Sugar-Plum Cake

A child's dream.

2 9-inch yellow-cake layers
2 cups whipped cream

Frost cake layers with whipped cream; be sure sides and
   top are covered.

Place small amount whipped cream in icing bag.
Using rosette tip, pipe rosettes in a circle on top of cake.

Gum drops
Candied fruit
1 cup toasted almonds

Decorate each whipped-cream rosette with a gum drop or
   candied fruit.
Sprinkle cake with almonds.

Refrigerate until ready to serve.

Yield: 12 servings.

TUBE CAKES

Sponge Cake

6 eggs, separated
½ teaspoon salt
2 cups sugar

Beat egg whites, salt, and ½ cup sugar together until points form.

2¼ cups sifted cake flour
1¼ teaspoons baking powder

Sift together flour, baking powder, and 1 cup sugar.
Beat egg yolks with ½ cup sugar.

1 cup boiling water

2 teaspoons lemon rind or 1 teaspoon vanilla

Add water; stir only a little.
Add flour mixture all at once; stir until smooth.
Fold in egg-white mixture and lemon rind.

Bake in large ungreased tube pan in 325°F oven 50 to 60 minutes.

Yield: large tube cake.

Marble Pound Cake

1 stick butter
½ cup shortening
3 eggs
2 cups sugar
3 cups cake flour
2 teaspoons baking powder
½ teaspoon salt
1 cup milk
1½ teaspoons vanilla
¼ teaspoon baking soda
¾ cup chocolate syrup

Cream butter and shortening well.

Add eggs one at a time.
Add sugar; beat well.
Add sifted dry ingredients alternately with milk and vanilla.

Mix baking soda into chocolate syrup; let stand awhile.
Add chocolate syrup to about 4 or 5 tablespoons batter; mix well.
Pour white and chocolate batters alternately into tube pan.
Cut through batter with knife.

Bake at 350°F approximately 60 minutes.

Yield: 1 tube cake.

Buttermilk Pound Cake

3 cups sugar
1 cup shortening
6 eggs, separated

2 teaspoons lemon extract

3 cups unsifted all-purpose
  flour
½ teaspoon salt
¼ teaspoon soda
1 cup buttermilk

Blend sugar and shortening.

Add egg yolks one at a time; blend well after each addition.
Add flavoring.

Sift dry ingredients together. Add to first mixture alternately with buttermilk. (Begin and end with dry ingredients.)

Beat egg whites until stiff; carefully fold into mixture.

Bake in greased and floured tube pan in 350°F oven 70 minutes. Be sure top of cake is firm. It will have a crunchy-like crust on top.

Yield: 1 tube cake.

Rum Cake

3 cups flour
½ teaspoon soda
½ teaspoon baking powder
1 teaspoon salt

1 cup shortening
2 cups sugar
4 eggs, beaten
1 teaspoon vanilla extract
1 teaspoon lemon extract
1 teaspoon rum extract
1 cup buttermilk

Rum Glaze

1 cup sugar
½ cup water
2 teaspoons rum extract

Sift flour, soda, baking powder, and salt.

Cream shortening and sugar.

Add eggs.
Add flavorings.

Add flour and buttermilk alternately.

Bake in tube pan 1 hour at 350°F.

Boil sugar in water to dissolve.

Add rum extract; set aside to cool.

Pour glaze over cake while cake is hot and still in pan. Cool cake before removing from pan.

Yield: 1 tube cake.

Angel Food Cake

Soft, white, and light as a feather.

1 cup sifted cake flour
1½ cups sugar
¼ teaspoon salt

Sift flour 4 times with ¾ cup of sugar and salt.

12 egg whites
1¼ teaspoons cream of tartar

Beat egg whites with cream of tartar until soft peaks form.
Add remaining sugar, 2 tablespoons at a time; beat well after each addition.
Sift ¼ cup flour mixture over egg whites. Fold in carefully.
Fold in remaining flour mixture by fourths.
Turn into 10-inch tube pan.

Bake in preheated 375°F oven 35 to 40 minutes or until cake tests done.

Invert pan on funnel; cool completely.

Remove cake from pan.

Toasted slivered almonds
Confectioners' sugar

Scatter almonds on top.
Sprinkle with confectioners' sugar.

Yield: 10-inch tube cake.

Angel Food Cake

LOAF CAKES

Carrot Cake

1½ cups flour
1½ cups sugar
1 teaspoon baking powder
1 teaspoon salt
½ teaspoon baking soda
½ teaspoon cinnamon
½ teaspoon nutmeg
½ teaspoon ginger
¾ cup cooking oil
3 eggs
3 teaspoons hot water
1 cup cooked mashed
  carrots (canned will do)
½ cup walnuts

Mix dry ingredients together in order given.

Add cooking oil, eggs, water, and carrots; stir until well-blended.

Add walnuts.
Pour batter into ungreased loaf or tube pan.

Bake at 350°F 45 minutes.

Yield: 8 to 10 servings.

Carrot Cake

Cardamom Cake

Cardamom Cake

4 cups flour	Sift flour and baking powder into large bowl.
3 teaspoons baking powder	
1¼ cups sugar	Add 1 cup sugar, cardamom, and salt; make well in center.
2 teaspoons cardamom	
½ teaspoon salt	
1 cup cream	Pour in cream; mix together gently.
¼ pound butter	Add melted and cooled butter; mix all together to a smooth dough.
	Make dough into loaf shape about 10 inches long; put on greased baking sheet.
Slivered almonds	Sprinkle almonds over top of dough.
1 teaspoon cinnamon	Mix cinnamon and ¼ cup sugar; sprinkle over top.
	Press topping into dough with your fingers.
	Bake at 400°F 45 minutes.
	Let cake cool.
	Slice into thick pieces.
	Yield: 12 or more slices.

Pound Cake

½ pound butter
2 cups sugar
4 eggs, separated

3 cups flour
3 teaspoons baking powder
1 cup milk
1 teaspoon vanilla
¼ teaspoon nutmeg
  (Be generous!)

Cream butter and sugar with electric beater.

Add egg yolks one at a time.
Beat egg whites until very stiff; set aside.

Combine flour and baking powder.
Add some flour mixture and some milk to creamed mix-
  ture; repeat until all milk has been used.
Add vanilla and nutmeg.
Fold in egg whites with rubber spatula, gently but firmly.

Pour into 2 greased 9 × 5-inch loaf pans.

Bake at 350°F 45 minutes or until cakes test dry.

Yield: Two 9 × 5-inch loaves.

Pound Cake

Date Cake

4 eggs
1½ cups brown sugar
⅔ cup shortening
3¼ cups flour
5 teaspoons baking powder
1 teaspoon salt
1 teaspoon cinnamon
½ teaspoon nutmeg
¾ cup milk
1½ cups chopped dates

Separate eggs.
Cream yolks, sugar, and shortening.

Mix and sift flour, baking powder, salt, cinnamon, and
  nutmeg.
Add dry mixture to first mixture alternately with milk.
Beat egg whites well; stir into mixture.

Add dates; mix well.
Turn into greased loaf pan.

Bake in 350°F oven 50 to 60 minutes.

Cool; frost as desired.

Yield: 1 loaf cake.

Golden Bundt Cake

This rich, moist cake needs no frosting and keeps well.

3 cups sugar 1 cup butter or margarine ½ cup shortening	Beat sugar, butter, and shortening until light and fluffy, about 5 minutes.
5 eggs	Beat in eggs, one at a time; beat well after each addition.
3 cups unsifted flour ¼ teaspoon salt	Mix flour and salt.
5-ounce can evaporated milk plus water to make 1 cup	Alternately add flour and milk, ending with flour.
2 tablespoons vanilla butter and nut flavoring	Fold in flavoring.

Bake in greased tube pan at 325°F 1 hour and 45 minutes, until done. Start in cold oven. Do not open door.

Remove from pan; cool on wire rack.

Yield: 10 to 12 servings.

Chocolate-Nut Kuchen

1 cup whole-wheat flour 1½ cups all-purpose flour 1 teaspoon salt 1 teaspoon baking soda	Sift flours, salt, and baking soda together.
½ cup honey ¼ cup butter or margarine, softened	Cream honey and butter.
1 egg, beaten ⅔ cup milk	Combine egg and milk.
	Add dry ingredients alternately with egg–milk mixture to honey butter.
½ cup chopped walnuts or hazelnuts ½ cup raisins (optional)	Stir in nuts and raisins. Pour batter into greased loaf pan.
	Bake at 350°F about 60 minutes or until done. Remove loaf from pan to cool.
1 6-ounce package semisweet chocolate chips	Melt chocolate chips. Brush top of loaf with melted chocolate. Cool; serve.

Yield: 8½ × 4½-inch loaf.

Easy Honey Cake

4 eggs, beaten
2 cups sugar
1 cup oil
1-pound jar honey
4¼ cups flour
2 teaspoons cloves
1 teaspoon nutmeg
1 teaspoon ginger
½ teaspoon salt
2 teaspoons baking powder
1 teaspoon baking soda
2 cups strong coffee

Beat eggs with sugar on high speed 10 minutes.
Add oil and honey.

Mix all dry ingredients together before adding alternately with the coffee.

Grease large tube pan.
Line with waxed paper.

Bake 1½ hours at 325°F in well-preheated oven.

Let cool upside down.

Yield: large tube cake.

Loaf Cake

1½ cups unsifted flour
2 teaspoons baking powder

Sift flour and baking powder together.

2 eggs
1 cup sugar
½ pint heavy cream, whipped
1 teaspoon vanilla or ½ teaspoon vanilla and ½ teaspoon lemon extract

Beat eggs until light.
Blend in sugar.
Add whipped cream, vanilla, and flour.

Bake in greased and floured loaf pan at 325°F about 1 hour. Keeps very well refrigerated.

Yield: 1 loaf cake.

Easy Orange Loaf Cake

1¾ cups plus 2 tablespoons sifted flour
1¼ cups sugar
2 teaspoons baking powder
½ teaspoon salt
2 large eggs
½ cup orange juice and grated rind of 1 orange
½ cup shortening, softened

Put all ingredients together in mixing bowl.
Beat at medium speed 4 minutes.

Pour into well-greased and floured 9 × 5 × 4-inch loaf pan.

Bake at 350°F 1 hour.

Yield: 9 × 5-inch loaf cake.

Banana Cake

4 tablespoons sour cream **1 teaspoon baking soda**	Combine sour cream and baking soda in bowl; let stand 5 minutes.
¼ pound margarine **1½ cups sugar** **2 eggs**	Meanwhile, mix margarine, sugar, and eggs in another bowl. Add sour-cream mixture to this mixture.
2 large or 3 medium bananas, mashed **1½ cups flour** **1 teaspoon vanilla**	Add bananas; mix. Add vanilla and flour gradually; mix well. Pour into greased and floured loaf pan. Bake 1 hour at 350°F. Yield: 1 loaf cake.

Normandy Sand Cake

This delicate cake, flavored with Madeira, dates back to Victorian times.

1½ cups cake flour, sifted **1 teaspoon baking powder** **⅛ teaspoon nutmeg**	Sift flour, baking powder, and nutmeg together.
½ cup unsalted butter, softened **1 cup sugar** **3 eggs** **6 tablespoons Madeira** **½ teaspoon grated lemon rind**	Cream butter and sugar together, using electric mixer at medium speed, 5 minutes or until thick and creamy. Add eggs one at a time; beat well after each addition. Add flour mixture alternately with Madeira, beginning and ending with flour mixture; beat well after each addition. Stir in lemon rind. Pour batter into well-greased and floured loaf pan. Bake in a preheated 350°F oven 25 to 30 minutes or until cake tests done. Let cake cool in pan 5 minutes, then turn out onto rack to cool completely.
Confectioners' sugar	Dust with sifted confectioners' sugar before serving. Yield: 6 to 8 servings.

CHEESECAKES

Soft Cheesecake

2 cups fine graham-cracker
    crumbs
4 tablespoons butter
4 tablespoons sugar

Blend crumbs with butter and 4 tablespoons sugar.
Press into bottom and sides of 9-inch springform pan.

Cheese Filling

2 8-ounce packages cream
    cheese
1 cup granulated sugar
½ teaspoon salt
5 egg yolks
1 pint sour cream
1 teaspoon vanilla
1 tablespoon lemon juice
5 stiffly beaten egg whites

Beat cheese to soften.

Add 1 cup sugar and salt; cream well.

Add unbeaten egg yolks; stir just to blend.
Add sour cream, vanilla and lemon juice.
Fold into stiffly beaten whites by hand.

Pour into crumb-lined pan.

Bake at 300°F 1 hour.

Turn off oven.
Let cake remain in oven 1 hour with door closed; ½ hour
    with door open.
Remove from oven.
Let stand away from draft.
Cool thoroughly.
Refrigerate overnight.

Yield: 9-inch cheesecake.

Orange Cheesecake

Have all ingredients at room temperature.

½ cup margarine
¾ cup granulated sugar
3 tablespoons milk
1 cup all-purpose flour
4 eggs
½ teaspoon baking powder
1 teaspoon grated orange
   rind

2 8-ounce packages cream
   cheese
1 tablespoon flour
3 tablespoons thawed frozen
   orange-juice concentrate
1½ cups milk

Fresh orange slices for
   garnish

Combine margarine, ¼ cup sugar, 3 tablespoons milk, 1 cup flour, 1 egg, baking powder, and orange rind. Mix until well-blended.

Spread mixture in well-greased 10-inch springform pan.

Cream remaining sugar and cream cheese until fluffy.
Add 3 eggs; beat in.
Stir in 1 tablespoon flour, orange-juice concentrate, and 1½ cups milk. Beat until smooth.
Pour batter over dough.

Bake 1 hour at 300°F.

Remove from oven.
Cool completely before removing sides of pan.

Garnish with fresh orange slices.

Yield: 16 servings.

Orange Cheesecake

Chilled Cheesecake

3 tablespoons melted butter
¾ cup graham-cracker crumbs
Sugar
¼ teaspoon cinnamon
¼ teaspoon nutmeg

Combine butter, graham-cracker crumbs, 2 tablespoons sugar, cinnamon, and nutmeg in bowl.
Press ½ cup crumb mixture into 8- or 9-inch springform pan.

2 envelopes unflavored gelatin

Combine gelatin and ¾ cup sugar in medium saucepan.

2 eggs, separated
1 cup milk

Beat egg yolks.
Stir in milk gradually.
Stir into gelatin mixture.

Place over low heat.
Cook, stirring constantly, 3 to 5 minutes or until gelatin dissolves and mixture is slightly thickened.
Remove from heat.

1 teaspoon grated lemon rind
1 tablespoon lemon juice
1 teaspoon vanilla extract

Stir in lemon rind, lemon juice, and vanilla extract.

3 cups creamed cottage cheese
1 cup whipping cream, whipped

Beat cottage cheese with electric mixer at high speed 3 to 4 minutes or until smooth.
Stir into gelatin mixture.

Chill, stirring occasionally, until mixture mounds slightly when dropped from spoon.

Beat egg whites until stiff but not dry.
Add ¼ cup sugar gradually; beat until very stiff.
Fold into gelatin mixture, then fold in whipped cream.

Turn into prepared pan.
Sprinkle with remaining crumb mixture.
Chill 3 to 4 hours or until firm.
Loosen sides of pan with sharp knife; release springform.

An 8-cup loaf pan can be used instead of springform pan.
Grease loaf pan lightly.
Cut waxed paper to fit pan; line pan.

Invert onto serving plate to unmold; remove waxed paper.

Yield: 12 servings.

Chilled Cheesecake

Old-Fashioned Cheesecake

1½ cups flour (to start)
1½ teaspoons baking powder
⅓ cup oil
½ cup sugar
2 eggs

Mix flour, baking powder, oil, sugar, and eggs together.
Add additional flour until dough is dry enough to handle comfortably.
Divide unevenly, saving smaller piece for top crust.
Roll out bottom crust; shape it up sides of 9-inch-square pan.

Cheese Filling

½ pound farmer cheese
½ pound cottage cheese
2 eggs
1 tablespoon sour cream
⅓ cup sugar or to taste
2 to 3 tablespoons challah crumbs

Mix ingredients for cheese filling together.
Put cheese filling on top of bottom crust.

Roll out top crust. Cover cheese filling.
Make a few air holes with fork in several places.

Bake about 1 hour in 300°F oven.

Yield: 9-inch cheesecake.

53

ROLLED CAKES

Pistachio Cake Roll

5 large eggs
1 ¾ cups granulated sugar
½ teaspoon salt
2 teaspoons vanilla
1 ¼ cups all-purpose flour

Beat 5 large eggs until light and fluffy.
Gradually add 1 cup sugar, salt, and 1 teaspoon vanilla.
　　Beat until mixture begins to thicken.
Fold in flour, small portion at a time.

Pour mixture into greased and waxed, lined jelly pan.

Bake in 350°F oven 20 minutes or until done.

Remove cake from oven.
Turn onto a powdered-sugar-dusted cloth.
Remove paper and roll jelly-roll fashion.
Wrap ends of towel under cake; allow to cool in towel.

2 tablespoons cornstarch

Combine ¾ cup sugar and cornstarch in top of double
　　boiler.

3 eggs
1 cup milk
½ cup half-and-half
2 to 3 drops green food
　coloring
½ cup butter

Beat 3 eggs until fluffy. Add to sugar mixture; beat well to
　　combine.
Stir in milk and half-and-half; cook over double boiler until
　　thick.
Remove from heat.
Stir in coloring, butter, and 1 teaspoon vanilla.
Cool.

½ cup chopped pistachio
　nuts

Unfold cake; spread with cooled filling.
Sprinkle chopped pistachio nuts over cream filling.
Reroll cake.
Chill.

2 cups whipped cream
½ cup whole pistachio nuts

Frost chilled cake roll with whipped cream. Decorate top
　　with whole pistachio nuts.
Refrigerate.
Yield: 12 servings.

Chocolate Roll

4 egg whites ½ cup sugar 4 egg yolks, beaten 4 tablespoons cold water	Beat egg whites until stiff. Add sugar gradually, beating constantly. Add egg yolks and water.
4 tablespoons cocoa 1 cup flour 1 teaspoon baking powder ½ teaspoon salt	Mix and sift cocoa, flour, baking powder, and salt. Fold into first mixture.
	Line long shallow pan with greased paper. Pour batter into pan. Bake in 400°F oven 15 to 20 minutes. Turn out onto damp cloth; cool slightly.
1 cup cream ½ teaspoon vanilla 2 tablespoons confectioners' sugar	Beat cream stiff with vanilla and confectioners' sugar; spread on cake. Roll like jelly roll. Sprinkle with powdered sugar. Yield: 1 cake roll.

Jelly Roll

2 eggs ⅞ cup sugar Grated rind of 1 lemon	Beat eggs. Add sugar; beat well. Add rind.
1 cup flour 1½ teaspoons baking powder ¼ teaspoon salt 3 tablespoons milk	Sift flour with baking powder and salt. Add alternately with milk to first mixture.
	Pour into shallow pan, about 14 × 10 inches, lined with waxed paper. Bake in 350°F oven 15 to 20 minutes. Turn out onto damp cloth.
Jelly	Spread with jelly; roll up. Wrap in waxed paper; cool.
Confectioners' sugar	Sprinkle with confectioners' sugar just before serving. Yield: 14 × 10-inch jelly roll.

Pineapple-Cherry Roll-In-One

Preheat oven to 375°F.

3 tablespoons margarine
¾ cup light brown sugar
1 (20-ounce) can crushed
   pineapple, drained
¼ cup maraschino cherries,
   chopped, drained

Melt margarine in 15 × 10 × 1-inch jelly-roll pan.
Sprinkle brown sugar evenly over margarine.
Cover with pineapple and cherries.

3 eggs (room temperature)
¾ cup sugar
3 tablespoons orange juice
1 teaspoon vanilla
½ teaspoon almond extract

Beat eggs until light and fluffy.
Beat in sugar a little at a time. Beat well.
Add juice and flavorings; beat a few seconds.

¾ cup flour, sifted
1 teaspoon baking powder
½ teaspoon salt

Sift flour, baking powder, and salt together. Fold in
   carefully by hand or at low speed on mixer.
Pour into pan covering pineapple.

Bake 15 minutes.

Turn out on tea towel that has been dusted with confec-
   tioners' sugar.
Roll up from short end.
Cool in towel.

Yield: 12 servings.

COFFEE CAKES

Sherry Caramel Coffee Cake

This Sherry Caramel Coffee Cake is best served lightly warm. It can be frozen and reheated.

4 cups biscuit mix
Measure biscuit mix into large bowl.

⅓ cup packed light brown sugar
Blend in brown sugar and spices.

1½ teaspoons cinnamon

¼ teaspoon nutmeg

1 large egg
In another bowl beat egg.

¼ cup sherry
Combine sherry and milk with egg. Add this mixture and melted butter to dry ingredients in bowl.

1 cup milk

6 tablespoons butter or margarine, melted
Beat with electric mixer 3 or 4 minutes, until smooth.

Grease 9-inch-square cake pan or round pan to hold 8-cup size.

Spread ½ batter into prepared cake pan.

Caramel Crunch Topping
Sprinkle with half of Caramel Crunch Topping.

Spoon rest of batter mixture on top. Carefully spread with spatula.

Sprinkle remaining topping over batter.

Bake in 350°F oven 30 to 35 minutes, until cake is done.

Yield: 9-inch coffee cake.

Caramel Crunch Topping

½ cup packed light brown sugar
Put sugar, rind, and butter into small bowl.

1 teaspoon grated lemon rind
Mix with fingers until fine crumbs.

2 tablespoons soft butter

⅓ cup chopped nutmeats (any kind)
Add nutmeats.

Superb Coffee Cake

½ pound butter or
  margarine
1¼ cups sugar
2 eggs, beaten
1 cup sour cream
1 teaspoon vanilla
2 cups flour
1 teaspoon baking powder
½ teaspoon baking soda

Cream butter and sugar.

Add eggs, sour cream, and vanilla; beat well.

Gradually add sifted flour, baking powder, and baking
  soda.

Place ½ mixture in bottom of pan.
Sprinkle with ½ of topping mixture.
Repeat with balance.
Bake in preheated 350°F oven until knife comes out clean.
Sprinkle with confectioners' sugar while still warm.

Cool 15 to 20 minutes before cutting.

Yield: one 9-inch tube cake or two 8-inch-square cakes.

Cinnamon Topping

½ cup brown sugar
2 tablespoons flour
2 teaspoons cinnamon
½ cup chopped nuts
  (optional)

Mix ingredients together.

For tube pan, use 9-inch springform. Bake at least 1 hour.
Can also be made in two 8-inch-square pans. Bake about
  40 minutes.

Cake freezes very well.

Great Coffee Cake

1 cup white sugar
1 cup brown sugar
2½ cups flour
1 teaspoon cinnamon
1 teaspoon nutmeg
1 teaspoon salt
¾ cup cooking oil
1 beaten egg
1 cup buttermilk
1 teaspoon baking soda

Mix together sugars, flour, cinnamon, nutmeg, salt, and oil.
Remove ¾ cup of mixture for crumbs.

Add egg, buttermilk, and baking soda to remaining batter.

Put in ungreased 8 × 12-inch pan; sprinkle crumbs on top.
  Bake at 350°F 45 minutes.

Yield: 8 × 12-inch coffee cake.

ICINGS

Fluffy Coconut Icing

2 egg whites
½ teaspoon cream of tartar
2½ tablespoons cold water
¾ cup sugar
Pinch of salt

In top of double boiler mix all ingredients except coconut, cream, and vanilla.
Put pot on top of boiling water in bottom half of double boiler; beat constantly with beaters 7 full minutes.
Cool.

½ pint whipping cream
1 teaspoon vanilla
1 package or 2 cans coconut

Whip the cream separately; fold into mixture.
Add vanilla.
Add ½ of coconut; fold in.
Put on cooled cake. Sprinkle remaining coconut on icing between layers, around sides, and on top.

Keep refrigerated.

Yield: enough for 9-inch layer cake.

Coffee-Cream Frosting

2 teaspoons freeze-dried coffee
¼ cup boiling water

Dissolve coffee in boiling water; reserve.

½ cup margarine
½ cup shortening
5 cups powdered sugar, sifted
1 egg, beaten

Cream margarine and shortening until fluffy.

Beat in 2½ cups sugar until smooth.

Add egg; mix well.
Add remaining sugar; beat until frosting is well-mixed and free from lumps.
Add coffee; beat until frosting becomes light and fluffy.

Yield: approximately 3 cups.

Chocolate Frosting

3 (1-ounce) squares
   unsweetened chocolate
⅓ cup butter
3 cups sifted confectioners'
   sugar
½ cup milk
1 teaspoon vanilla
¼ teaspoon salt

Melt chocolate and butter in top of double boiler. Remove from heat.

With electric mixer blend in sugar, milk, vanilla, and salt.

Frosting will be slightly thin, so place bowl in ice water and beat until of spreading consistency.

Yield: enough for 9-inch layer cake.

Decorating Icing

1 pound powdered sugar
Pinch of salt
¼ cup cold water
½ pound shortening (not
   butter or margarine)
Food coloring
¼ teaspoon vanilla

Cream sugar, salt, and water. Add shortening and flavoring.
If too soft, add more shortening.
If too stiff, add a little water.
This must have consistency to hold shape when worked through pastry tubes.
Add coloring, a little at a time, until right tint is obtained.

Left-over icing can be frozen for future use or stored in refrigerator up to 2 weeks.

Uncooked Chocolate Frosting

3 cups confectioners' sugar
5 tablespoons cocoa or 3
   squares chocolate, melted
1 stick less 1 tablespoon
   butter
1 tablespoon light corn
   syrup
1 teaspoon vanilla
Evaporated milk

Beat all but milk slowly with electric beater.
Add enough milk to make an easy spreading frosting; beat until very smooth.

Yield: enough for 2-layer cake.

Creamy Uncooked Chocolate Icing

2¼ cups unsifted confec-
    tioners' sugar
¼ cup hot water
4 squares unsweetened
    chocolate, melted
1 egg, unbeaten
6 tablespoons softened
    butter

Add sugar and water to chocolate.

Beat in egg.
Add butter a tablespoon at a time; beat well after each
    addition.

Yield: enough for two 9-inch layers.

Mocha Frosting

3 cups confectioners' sugar
¼ cup cocoa
¼ teaspoon cinnamon
⅔ cup soft margarine
2 tablespoons cold coffee
2 teaspoons vanilla
1 teaspoon flavoring

Sift together sugar, cocoa, and cinnamon.

Cream the margarine.
Add sugar mixture, coffee, and flavorings. Beat a few
    minutes until smooth.

Frost cooled cake. (Cake must be cool or margarine
    separates.)

Yield: enough for 14 × 9-inch pan cake or 9-inch 3-layer
    cake.

Coconut Frosting

½ cup coconut
5 tablespoons brown sugar
3 tablespoons melted butter
2 tablespoons heavy cream
½ teaspoon vanilla

Mix all ingredients together.
Spread frosting on warm cake.
Place in oven 5 minutes or until top sets.

Yield: enough for 8 × 8-inch cake. Can be doubled for
    layer cake.

Fluffy Frosting

1 cup sugar
¼ teaspoon cream of tartar
⅛ teaspoon salt
1 tablespoon light corn
   syrup
⅓ cup water
1 egg white

¼ teaspoon vanilla extract

Bring sugar, cream of tartar, salt, corn syrup, and water to
   boil; cook until sugar dissolves.

Add to unbeaten egg white; beat constantly with electric
   beater until frosting is of spreading consistency.
Add vanilla.

Yield: enough for 8-inch layer cake.

Vanilla Cream-Cheese Frosting

3 ounces cream cheese
½ cup soft butter
1 tablespoon vanilla
2 cups confectioners' sugar

Cream cream cheese, butter, and vanilla until fluffy.
Add sugar a little at a time. Beat until spreadable, then ice
   cake.

Yield: enough for 8-inch 3-layer cake.

Fluffy White Frosting

Successful cooked frosting depends on all *ingredients being at room temperature and on following
directions.*

2 egg whites
¾ cup granulated sugar
⅓ cup light corn syrup
2 tablespoons warm water
¼ teaspoon salt

Combine all ingredients in 4-quart ovenproof glass mixing
   bowl.
Beat 1 minute on high with electric mixer.
Place bowl over boiling water. (Be sure bottom of bowl
   does not touch metal of pan with boiling water.)
Beat *exactly* 7 minutes.
Remove from boiling water.
Beat until frosting stands in peaks.

Note: Coloring or flavoring can be added after frosting is
   removed from boiling water.

Yield: approximately 4 cups.

INDEX

63